DASH Diet Slow Cooker Recipes

60 Delicious Low Sodium Slow Cooker Recipes

By Renee Sanders

DASH Diet Slow Cooker Recipes

Published by Awesome Life Resources. 2015

Ebook ASIN: B00TQYTTFI

Paperback ISBN: 978-1508657743

Table of Contents

BREAKFAST & BRUNCH RECIPES

- Overnight slow cooker oatmeal
- Crock pot stone ground grits
- Homemade granola
- Slow cooker Cinnamon Casserole
- Mix trail porridge
- Slow cooker baked apple
- Fruit Compote
- Baked French toast
- Slow cooker Farina porridge
- Cranberry oatmeal and toasted almonds

MAIN DISH RECIPES

- Slow cooker lentil chilies & chickpea
- Slow cooker sweet potato & vegetable curry
- Slow cooker quinoa with roasted poblanos
- Slow cooker sweet potato chili
- Crock pot bean and quinoa
- Slow cooker Mediterranean stew
- Black bean & rice in slow cooker
- Cauliflower chickpea curry
- Slow cooker vegetarian chili
- Barbecued Tofu with Vegetables
- Vegan chickpea slow cooking stew
- Red bean & rice in slow cooker
- Crock pot spicy chickpea curry
- Slow cooker vegetable stew

Slow cooked veggie chili

Mint rice with slowed coked lentils

Blackeyed peas & Okra in a crock pot

Vegan Spaghetti squash

Indian style lentils

Potato & kidney bean crock pot curry

SIDE DISH RECIPES

Garlic parmesan potatoes

Yellow squash

Glazed carrots

Sweet potato casserole

Garlic mashed potatoes

Slow cooked green bean

Root vegetables in a crock pot

Mushroom-Barley Risotto

Onions caramalized in the crock pot

Slow cooking loaded baked potatoes

DESSERT RECIPES

Slow cooked apple crisp

Crock pot Fudge

Crock pot Rice Pudding

Sugar candied cinnamon & almonds

Crock pot banana foster

Donut Bread pudding

Slow cooked tapioca pudding

Crock pot nutella chocolate chip cake

FREE BONUS!

To help you start your DASH diet and stay committed to your diet plan, I've put together a DASH Diet Hamper which includes the following:

a. Audio version of the Amazon Bestseller book **"Blood Pressure Solution" by Jessica Robbins**
b. **7 day vegetarian meal plan** for DASH Diet
c. DASH Diet Shopping List
d. Tips to get started with the DASH Diet
e. Tips to reduce your sodium intake
f. Sodium Content Chart of various foods

Additional Bonus!

Receive the first copies of all my diet and cookbooks as soon as they get published for FREE!

Get Access to the FREE DASH Diet Hamper HERE:
http://dietcookbooks.co/dashdiet/

Introduction

Thank you for downloading my book DASH diet slow cooker recipes. This book contains the steps and techniques of how to utilize the adaptability and comfort of slow cooker which is also commonly called as Crock Pot. It highlights those points which would benefit anyone about slow cooking and also the benefits about it. This book also provides some amazing recipes from hot pouring soups to morning breakfast & brunch to some yummy main dishes and side dishes and some delicious dessert recipes which are not only inclining towards healthy weight management but also leading towards a healthy lifestyle. The book would be a wonderful treat for vegetarians as all the recipes are 100% vegetarian.

Slow cooking or Crock pot recipes involve a lot of patience but the effort is not only satisfactory but also worth the time.

In this book, I've carefully handpicked 60 crock pot recipes from among the best of recipes in my kitchen diary. All the recipes in this book adhere to the recommendations prescribed by the DASH diet. This diet mainly focuses on how to keep your blood pressure under control by eating low sodium based foods. As this diet promotes healthy eating, people without high blood pressure also follow it because of the numerous benefits it offers like weight reduction and protection against diabetes, cancer, osteoporosis, cardiovascular diseases, stroke etc.

For the 5th year in a row, DASH Diet has been ranked as the #1 diet among the 35 diets evaluated and ranked by US News & World Report. According to the experts in their panel, "To be top-rated, a diet has to be relatively easy to follow, nutritious, safe and effective for weight loss and against diabetes and heart disease". Studies sponsored by the National Heart, Lung, and Blood Institute (NHLBI) have proven that DASH diet reduces high blood pressure, which in turn lowers the risk of developing cardiovascular disease.

What is DASH diet?

This chapter is taken from my <u>DASH Diet for Vegetarians</u> book.

The DASH (Dietary Approach to Stop Hypertension) diet is prescribed as the best diet to lower the blood pressure by eating less sodium. Apart from avoiding sodium, the main key ingredients that are involved in this diet are foods rich in potassium, calcium and magnesium which are connected to lowering blood pressure. This dietary goal can be achieved by combining fresh fruits and vegetables, low fat and non-fat dairy products, nuts, legumes and whole grains in the daily diet. Additionally, DASH diet helps in reducing cholesterol, which in turn helps in weight loss and reduces the risk of heart strokes, osteoporosis, several types of cancer, kidney stones and diabetes.

Guidelines to be followed while dash dieting.

No Special foods

Unlike other diet plans, DASH diet is very easy to follow as it does not suggest any special foods to be consumed. By making small changes to your normal diet and the cooking methods, you can easily follow the guidelines of this diet.

Foods to be included

Vegetable and fruit consumption has to be increased, especially lot of dark-green vegetables, tomatoes, beans, carrots, broccoli and peas – at least 4-5 servings per day. Examples: apricots, bananas, dates, grapes, oranges, grapefruit, mangoes, melons, peaches, pineapples, prunes, strawberries, tangerines

Refined grains have to be totally replaced and whole grains should be taken as whole grains contain more fiber and are packed with nutrients – 6-8 servings per day.

Low fat & non fat dairy products like skimmed milk, buttermilk and fat free yogurt can be consumed- 2-3 servings per day.

4-5 servings per day of nuts and seeds like peanuts, walnuts, sunflower seeds, almonds etc are beneficial.

Lean meats like skinless chicken, sea foods etc. can be consumed. Vegetarians can opt for other plant-based sources of protein like soy and tofu.

Food to be avoided

It is advised to reduce the food consumption of refined food grains that contain fats, added sugars and salts (sodium).

Red meats, aerated sugary beverages and sweets like jelly, jam, sorbet, maple syrup etc. should be avoided- not more than 5 servings per week.

Do not consume more than 2-3 servings of oils and fats per day. This includes the oil used for cooking, salad dressing, sandwich spreads etc. Avoid unsaturated fats and transfats as much as possible.

Alcohol consumption should be restricted. Men shouldn't take more than 2 servings of alcohol per day and women shouldn't consume more than 1 serving per day.

Balance the calories with exercise to manage weight

Try to reduce weight if you are overweight or obese and maintain a healthy weight by a constant improvement in eating healthy food and also by involving in various physical activities. The American Heart Association recommends 30 minutes of exercise per day, 5 times week, in addition to following the diet plan.

It's also advised to balance your calorie intake depending on the stage of your life cycle – E.g. pregnancy, older age etc. and the type of your lifestyle- sedentary, moderate or active.

DASH Diet Aim

The DASH (Dietary Approaches to Stop Hypertension) eating plan is recommended to help lower blood pressure by the National Institutes of Health and most physicians. The DASH diet is rich in fruits, vegetables, low fat or non-fat dairy, and also includes grains, especially whole grains; lean meats, fish and poultry; nuts and beans. In addition to lowering blood pressure, it has been shown to lower cholesterol. It is an extremely healthy way of eating, designed to be flexible enough to meet the lifestyle and food preferences of most people.

DASH diet: Sodium levels

Standard DASH diet - You can consume up to 2,300 milligrams (mg) of sodium a day.

Lower sodium DASH diet - You can consume up to 1,500 mg of sodium a day.

Both versions of the DASH diet aim to reduce the amount of sodium in your diet compared with what you might get in a more traditional diet, which can amount to a whopping 3,500 mg of sodium a day or more.

The standard DASH diet meets the recommendation from the Dietary Guidelines for Americans to keep daily sodium intake to less than 2,300 mg a day. The lower sodium version of the diet matches the recommendation to reduce sodium to 1,500 mg a day if you're 51 and older, black, or have hypertension, diabetes or chronic kidney disease. The American Heart Association recommends 1,500 mg as an upper limit for all adults. If you aren't sure what sodium level is right for you, it is best to consult your doctor.

DASH diet recommendations for a 2000 Calorie Diet plan would be as follows:

Total fat	27% of calories
Saturated fat	6% of calories
Protein	18% of calories
Carbohydrate	55% of calories
Cholesterol	150 mg
Sodium	2,300 mg*
Potassium	4,700 mg
Calcium	1,250 mg
Magnesium	500 mg
Fiber	30 g

An easier way to track your diet would be to keep a check on the number of servings of each food group. Here is the DASH diet recommendation for a 1600 cal/day and a 2000 cal/day diet plan.

	Servings per Day	
Food Group	**1600 Calories**	**2000 Calories**
Grains & Grain Products	6	7-8
Vegetables	3-4	4-5
Fruits	4	4-5
Low Fat or Fat-free Dairy Foods	2-3	2-3
Meats/ poultry/	1-2	2 or less

fish/ vegetarian alternatives		
Nuts, seeds, dry beans	3 per week	4-5 per week
Fast & oils	2	2-3
Sweets	2 per week	5 per week

Slow Cooking: The Basics First

Working of a slow cooker

It's a cold day and the worst thing you could think of is to thrall over the stove to cook a meal. Luckily, a decent meal is already prepared and once you enter your home, you are greeted by the aroma of the stew drifting in the air, tempting you to have a delicious dinner.

Even though nobody is around the cooking process, thanks to the slow cooker, the meal would be ready by the time you are home. The small electrical countertop appliance which was a staple household appliance 40 years back is based on the slow cooking process. The idea of slow cooking is very simple - take all the ingredients needed for a recipe and add it to the container, set the temperature and allow it to cook slowly. The cooking can be unattended, which is a huge advantage over stovetop cooking. Slow cooking happens when the heating element in the cooker heats the ingredients in the container to a steady low heat temperature over a prolonged period of time. This method was around since centuries and was widely accepted in the 1970's kitchen. But when electric oven came into existence, slow cookers were left behind as people started using the oven as a resource to cook food.

However, thanks to the concept of slow healthy cooking, the slow cooker is back to existence with a wide variety of recipes to choose from. Many books are in the market now focusing on the benefits of slow cooking with some delicious and healthy recipes which can be cooked in a slow cooker.

Slow cooking Equipment

Slow cooker came into existence into the household kitchen in the early 1960s and became a huge hit instantly. Especially for the working women, this became a great asset as the meal is prepared at one shot and would be cooked while they are away from home and ready by the time they reach home.

Slow cooker-parts

An outer exterior

An inner container

A glass lid.

Design of the equipment:

A basic unit of slow cooker contains a round lid or oval pot made of ceramic or porcelain, surrounded with metal which contains an electric heating element. The lid is mostly made of glass and provides low-pressure seal to the atmosphere. This unit is different from the normal pressure cooker and has no danger of immediate pressure release.

The outer part of the cooker is made of metal and contains heat coils which are accountable for cooking food. The inner container is generally made of ceramic and sits on the metal heating element of the outer case. In some of the models; the inner case can be removed easily. The third piece is the glass lid that fits the crock pot tightly.

The cooking process is generally based on the heat and time. When the crock pot is switched on, the heal coil which is present in the outer case started getting heated, transfers the heat between the walls of the inner container and allows the food present in the container to cook slowly by transferring continuous heat slowly for long hours until the food is cooked thoroughly and properly.

As the food cooks, it releases the steam which the lid of the crock pot starts captivating within it which in turn helps the food to be moist throughout the cooking process. Hence, the lid of the slow cooker plays a vital role. Usually, the cooker has three main temperature parts, High, Low and Off. But, since the technology has developed, the cooker now is coming with different settings which allow the food to be warm at the required temperature.

Benefits of slow cooking

Saves time: Using is a slow cooker can be benefitted by saving lots of time and also involves healthy cooking. By just gathering all the required ingredients in the container, one can stay away from kitchen and can be involved in other activities not bothering about the cooking process. Once the food is cooked, the device automatically is switched to a warm temperature allowing the food to be fresh all through.

No extra cleaning: This is one of the best appliances for busy people as they can just assemble the ingredients in a single container and allow it to cook. There is no headache of many dishes in the kitchen to clean.

Economic usage: Slow cooker is the best and the smartest choice as it can be used economically. As you are saving time and money, it's not necessary to give up the flavors of food. The ingredients or the vegetables can be cooked thoroughly by adding enough spices to give the required amount of taste to the food.

User friendly: Thanks to the new technology, now-a-days, the slow cooker is programmed well and allows the settings to be changed to high or low temperature automatically as and when the meal is being prepared.

What can be cooked in slow cooker?

Vegetables can be cooked in a slow cooker, but one has to ensure to cut all the vegetables in a uniform size so that it can cook evenly. Vegetables take a little longer time to cook than meats so, it's very important to arrange them properly at the bottom of the pot.

The best meals that can be cooked in slow cooker are the stews and soups. As these taste much better when they are boiled or cooked for longer time.

Dips and spreads are another group that be cooked well in a slow cooker. The low heat produced by the slow cooker keeps the ingredients warm inside without burning.

Grains can also be cooked wonderfully using the slow cooking method. Oatmeal can be cooked overnight and can be eaten in the morning during breakfast with healthy nutrients. Breads can also be baked; another surprise category is the desserts-delicious desserts can be cooked without any hassle.

Tips for slow cooker meals

Uniform cut: Always choose to cut uniformly so that the ingredients involved in cooking are cooked properly and evenly.

Keep the lid closed: The lid of the slow cooker has to be closed throughout the cooking process. Each time you remove the lid, the cooking process time will be extended for 10-15minutes more. It is not necessary to stir the ingredients as it simply slows down the process.

Protect your pot: Always ensure to get the ceramic pot to a room temperature before running it under cold water to avoid any cracks.

No to frozen foods: Frozen foods have to be avoided as the ingredients in the food will take them to a danger zone where bacteria can prosper. Always ensure the vegetables or the meat is at a room temperature and is softened before cooking.

Keep away from overcrowding: Do not overcrowd the pot by adding more and more ingredients. Ensure the pot is half or two-thirds filled. Use a bigger pot while cooking more ingredients and see the lid sits fitted on to the pot correctly.

Add dairy product at last: Add the dairy products like milk, cream curd or yogurt at the last 15minutes of cooking process as it may curdle and break down.

Last minute Flavors: Try sprinkling some extra flavors like fresh herbs and spices at the end of the cooking process and can bring in the enticing flavors and richness to the food. Other finishing products are, grated parmesan cheese, olive oil, garlic sautéed or any hot sauce.

SOUP RECIPES

Crock pot Butternut squash & quinoa soup

Ingredients

1 yellow onion (medium, chopped)

3 lbs butternut squash (peeled, cut into ½-inch cubes)

1 cup quinoa (rinsed and drained)

15 ozs cannellini beans

15 ozs black beans

141/2 ozs diced tomatoes (undrained)

2 tsp cumin

11/2 tsp hot chili powder

1/4 tsp garlic powder

1/8 tsp cinnamon

6 cups low sodium vegetable broth

Chopped cilantro (fresh, for serving)

Direction:

Place all the ingredients in a slow cooker and cook for one hour on high and low for 5-8 hours. Remove and sprinkle fresh cilantro. Serves 4.

Slow cooker Olive garden Soup

Ingredients

4 cups low sodium vegetable stock

11/2 cups water

29 ozs diced tomatoes

1 cup diced celery (3 stalks)

1 cup carrots (diced, 2 carrots)

1 cup diced yellow onion (1 small)

1 tbsp fresh parsley

2 tsp dried basil

1 tsp dried oregano

1/2 tsp dried thyme

1/2 tsp rosemary (dried crushed)

2 bay leaves

1/2 tsp sugar

Ground black pepper

Salt

11/3 cups zucchini (diced, 1 small)

11/3 cups shell pasta

4 cloves garlic (minced)

15 ozs red kidney beans

15 ozs navy beans

141/2 ozs green beans (Italian, drained)

2 cups fresh spinach

Shredded romano cheese (Finely, for serving, Parmesan works too)

Directions:

Place vegetable stock, water, tomatoes, celery, carrots, onion, parsley, basil, oregano, thyme, rosemary, bay leaves and sugar to a 6 or 7-quart slow cooker. Season with salt and pepper to taste and cook on low heat 6 - 8 hours or high 3 - 4 hours. Add in zucchini, pasta, garlic, kidney beans and white beans and cook on high heat for an additional 30 - 40 minutes until pasta is tender. Stir in spinach and Italian green beans and cook several minutes until heated through. Serve warm topped with Romano cheese.

Slow cooker Red lentil Soup

Ingredients

1 tbsp olive oil

1 yellow onion

2 carrots

2 celery ribs

4 cloves garlic

2 tsp ground cumin

1/2 tsp cayenne pepper

11/2 tsp smoked paprika

4 cups red lentils

2 bay leaves

16 cups low sodium vegetable stock

Kosher salt

1 tbsp red wine vinegar

1 purple onion

1/3 cup coriander leaf

1 lemon

Directions:

Heat olive oil in a large pan over medium heat. When oil is shimmering, add onion, carrots, and celery and cook, stirring periodically, until vegetables start to soften, about 5 minutes. Add garlic and stir until fragrant for about 1 minute. Add in cumin, cayenne, and paprika, and continue cooking until fragrant. Transfer mixture to a slow cooker. Add lentils, bay leaves and 12 cups of stock. Season with about 1 teaspoon of salt, stir to combine, and cover. Set slow cooker to low and cook for 4 hours, stirring hourly and adding in additional broth as needed to maintain a loose, soup-like consistency. When the soup is done, discard bay leaves, transfer to a blender or food processor, and add vinegar. Adjust seasonings, if needed and purée until smooth. Ladle into bowls and top with red onion and cilantro, and serve with lemon wedges.

Butternut squash with maple roasted soup

Ingredients

1 chopped yellow onion

3 chopped carrots

1 butternut squash

1 chopped apples

28 ozs low sodium vegetable broth

1/2 tsp ground cinnamon

1/4 tsp ground nutmeg

2 tsp maple syrup

Ground black pepper

Salt

15 ozs garbanzo beans

1 tbsp canola oil

11/2 tsp pure maple syrup

1 tbsp brown sugar

1/4 tsp ground cinnamon

1/8 tsp salt

Directions:

Add the onion, carrots, butternut squash, and apple to the slow cooker. Pour the vegetable broth over all of the ingredients. Cook on low for 6 hours or on high for 3 1/2 to 4 hours. Once vegetables are cooked and soft, puree the soup using an immersion blender. Add the cinnamon, nutmeg, and maple syrup. Season with salt and pepper, to taste. If you don't have an immersion blender, you can transfer the soup to a blender (in batches) and puree until smooth. Pour the soup back into the slow cooker and season with spices and maple syrup. While the soup is cooking in the slow cooker, make the maple roasted chickpeas. Preheat the oven to 375 degrees F. Rinse and drain the chickpeas and pat dry with a towel. Remove the skins by rolling them on the towel. In a small bowl, combine the canola oil, maple syrup, brown sugar, cinnamon, and salt. Place the chickpeas on a large baking sheet. Pour the maple syrup mixture over the chickpeas and toss until chickpeas are well coated. Place in the oven and bake for 40-45 minutes, stirring every 15 minutes or so. Remove from the oven when chickpeas are crunchy. Pour soup into bowls and garnish with maple roasted chickpeas. Serve immediately.

Slow cooker Tomato spinach soup

Ingredients

10 ozs baby spinach

2 chopped carrots

2 celery ribs

1 onion (large, chopped)

1 garlic cloves (minced)

4 cups low sodium vegetable broth

1 diced tomatoes (28 ounce)

2 bay leaves

1 tbsp dried basil

1 tsp dried oregano

1/2 tsp red pepper flakes (crushed)

Directions:

Place all ingredients in a slow cooker. Cover and cook on high for 5 hours or low for 8-10 hours. Remove bay leaves, stir and serve.

Potato broccoli slow cooker soup

Ingredients

4 potatoes (peeled and cubed)

2 potatoes (peeled and diced)

1 head broccoli (diced)

1 onion (minced)

7 cups milk

2 tsp garlic powder

2 tsp fresh chives (minced)

2 cups instant potato flakes

1/4 cup dry bread crumbs

Directions:

Place the cubed potatoes, diced potatoes, broccoli, onion, milk, garlic powder, and chives in a slow cooker; cover, and cook on High for 4 hours. Stir the instant potato flakes and bread crumbs into the soup. Reduce heat to low for another 30 minutes. Serve hot.

Vegetable Quinoa Soup

Ingredients

2 diced onions

3 diced carrots

2 stalks diced celery

1 diced red bell pepper

1 diced green bell pepper

1 diced zucchini

2 cloves garlic (minced)

1 vegetable broth (carton, 32 ounces)

2 cups water

28 ozs crushed tomatoes

15 ozs cannellini beans (drained and rinsed)

15 ozs garbanzo beans (drained and rinsed)

1 lime (juiced)

2 tsp Italian seasoning

2 tsp nutritional yeast

Black pepper

3/4 cup quinoa

3 cups kale

Directions:

Place everything except quinoa and kale to the slow cooker. Cook for 3-4 hours on high or 6-8 hours on low. Add the quinoa and kale and cook for 30 – 60 minutes longer, or until the quinoa is fully cooked. Serve with oyster crackers or Parmesan cheese and enjoy!

Stunning vegetable crock pot soup

Stunning vegetable crockpot soup

Ingredients

4 carrots (thinly sliced)

5 stalks celery (sliced)

4 potatoes (cubed)

9 ozs frozen green beans

Onions (1 med., chopped)

2 cloves garlic (minced)

1 cup canned tomatoes (diced)

4 cups tomato juice

11/2 cups water

1 tbsp dried parsley

3/4 tsp dried oregano

1 tsp herb seasoning

Salt (to taste)

1 can red kidney bean

Directions:

Place all ingredients in crock pot insert. Cook on low for 8-10 hours or on high for 6 hours. Season with salt to taste. Just before serving, stir in kidney beans. Serve hot.

Slow cooker lentil soup

Ingredients

2 tsp olive oil

1 onion

3 cloves garlic (minced)

2 carrots

1 celery ribs

5 cups water (or stock, use vegetable stock for vegan/vegetarian)

1 cup green lentil

1 cup tomato sauce

2 tsp tomato paste

2 bay leaves

Salt

Pepper

2 tsp red wine vinegar

Directions:

Heat oil in a large pan, sauté onion, garlic, carrots and celery; cook about 5 minutes until onions are softened. Transfer vegetables to slow cooker. Add water or stock, lentils, tomato sauce, tomato paste, bay leaves, salt and pepper. Cook on low for 8-9 hours until lentils are tender. Remove bay leaves. Stir in vinegar just before serving.

Spicy carrot & pumpkin slow cooker soup

Ingredients

1 chopped onions

2 garlic (fat cloves)

2 tsp oil

2 chunks carrots

2 chunks potatoes

4 chunks pumpkin

3 tsp plain flour

1 tsp salt

1/2 tsp curry powder

1 pinch chilies (ground)

21/2 tsp paprika

1/4 tsp nutmeg

Pepper (a good grind)

3 cups vegetable stock

 Water

Fresh mint

Directions:

In a large pan heat the oil and add the onion and garlic. Cook until softened. Add the prepared vegetables and the flour and mix as well as you can, allowing the flour to absorb .Put the whole lot into the slow cooker. Add the spices, salt, pepper, stock and water and cook on high for 4 hours or low for 6 hours. When the vegetables are tender, purée or process the soup until smooth and return to the slow cooker to keep warm. Adjust the consistency and add some chopped mint.

BREAKFAST & BRUNCH RECIPES

Overnight slow cooker oatmeal

Ingredients

1/2 cup steel-cut oats

2 cups water

1/2 tsp cinnamon

1 tsp vanilla extract

1/2 cup dried cranberries

Pure maple syrup (for topping**)**

Directions:

Combine the oats, water, cinnamon and vanilla extract in a small, 1 or 2 quart slow cooker. Cook on low for 8 hours. Stir in the cranberries and maple syrup when serving.

Crock pot stone ground grits

Ingredients

11/2 cups grits (uncooked stone-ground yellow)

41/2 cups water

Freshly ground pepper

Salt

Directions:

Stir together grits and water in a 3-qt. slow cooker. Let it stand for 2 minutes, allowing grits to settle to bottom; tilt slow cooker slightly, and skim off solids using a fine wire-mesh strainer. Cover and cook on HIGH 2 1/2 to 3 hours or until grits are creamy and tender, stirring every 45 minutes. Season with salt and freshly ground pepper to taste.

Homemade granola

Ingredients

5 cups rolled oats

1/2 cup slivered almonds

1/4 tsp kosher salt

2/3 honey

1/3 cup coconut oil

1/2 cup chunky peanut butter

2 tsp cinnamon

1 tbsp vanilla

1 cup raisins

Directions:

Lightly grease the crock-pot with a teaspoon or so of oil. Add the oats, almonds and salt. In a large measuring cup or small glass bowl, combine the honey, oil, peanut butter, cinnamon and vanilla. Microwave for a minute, stir and microwave an additional 30 seconds as needed, to melt everything and allow it to combine smoothly. Pour the liquids over the oats in the crock pot and stir well to thoroughly coat. Place the lid on the crock pot, leaving it slightly vented. Cook on HIGH for about 2 hours, stirring every 30 minutes. Stir in the dried fruit right at the end. Spread the granola across a large baking sheet and let it cool before transferring to an airtight container. Enjoy! –

Slow cooker Cinnamon Casserole

Ingredients

24 ozs cinnamon rolls (tubes of, cut into quarters-divided)

1/2 cup whipping cream

3 tsp maple syrup

2 tsp vanilla

1 tsp cinnamon

1/4 tsp nutmeg

Directions:

Spray your crock with cooking spray. Place a layer of cinnamon roll pieces to cover the bottom of your slow cooker completely. Mix & beat cream, maple syrup, vanilla and spices until blended well. Pour evenly over the rolls in the slow cooker. Place remaining roll pieces on top and spoon one packet of icing evenly over rolls. Cover and cook on low for 2½ to 3 hours or until sides are golden and rolls are set. Drizzle remaining icing over top and serve warm.

Mix trail porridge

Ingredients

6 cups water

11/2 cups fresh cranberries (chopped)

3/4 cup pearl barley

3/4 cup light brown sugar

1/2 cup walnut pieces

6 tsp bulgur

6 tsp Corn

6 tsp millet

6 tsp maple syrup

1/2 tsp ground cinnamon

1/4 tsp salt

Directions:

Stir all the ingredients in a slow cooker until the maple syrup has dissolved and all the grains are moistened. Cover and cook on low for 6 hours, or until the porridge is creamy and the grains are tender.

Slow cooker baked apple

Slow cooker baked potato

Ingredients

6 green apples (medium to large)

1/4 cup raisins

1/4 cup honey

1 tsp cinnamon

6 tsp coconut oil (butter, or ghee)

Directions:

Using an apple corer or paring knife, cut around the core (about ¼ inches from the stem all the way around) but leave about half an inch at the bottom. Use the knife to 'drill out' the core. Divide raisins, honey, cinnamon, and coconut oil between the apples. Place apples in a crock pot and add ½ inch of water. Cook on low overnight and enjoy a hot breakfast in the morning!

Fruit Compote

Ingredients

2 cans sliced peaches

2 cans sliced pears

20 ozs pineapple chunks

151/4 ozs apricot halves

21 ozs cherry pie filling

Directions:

In a 5-qt. slow cooker, combine the peaches, pears, pineapple and apricots. Top with pie filling. Cover and cook on high for 2 hours or until heated through. Serve with a spoon.

Baked French toast

Ingredients

1 lb French bread (cut diagonally in 1 inch slices)

2 cups milk

11/2 cups cream (half-and-half)

2 tsp vanilla extract

1/4 tsp ground cinnamon

3/4 cup butter

11/3 cups brown sugar

3 tsp light corn syrup

Directions:

Take a baking dish and butter it all through. Arrange the slices of bread in the bottom. In a large bowl, beat together milk, cream, vanilla and cinnamon. Pour over bread slices, cover, and refrigerate overnight. The next morning, add them in the slow cooker and cook for high for 1 hr and low for 1 hr .In a small saucepan, combine butter, brown sugar and corn syrup; heat until bubbling. Pour over bread. Place it again the slow cooker and bake for 30mints.

Slow cooker Farina porridge

Ingredients

1/2 cup cream of wheat (or 1/2 cup farina)

1/3 cup wheat cereal

41/2 cups water

1 pinch salt

Directions:

Combine all the ingredients in a slow cooker. Cover and cook on LOW for 7-9 hours, or overnight, until creamy. Stir a few times with a whisk during cooking. Scoop into bowls and serve with milk and brown sugar.

Cranberry oatmeal and toasted almonds

Ingredients

3/4 cup sliced almonds

11/2 cups steel-cut oats (or rolled)

3 cups almond milk

1 cup water

1 tsp cinnamon

1/2 tsp salt

1/4 cup ground flax

1 tsp pure vanilla extract

3/4 cup dried cranberries

1/4 cup pure maple syrup

Directions:

Place almonds in a large sauce pan with no oil. Stir frequently for 5 minutes while almonds toast. Remove from pan and place in airtight container. Place oats, milk, water cinnamon, salt and flax in slow cooker. Cook on lowest setting for 7 hours. If you don't have a programmable slow cooker, Put in low setting for 6 hours and it can go straight to warm. Before serving, stir well and add cranberries, toasted almonds, maple syrup and vanilla. Stir again.

MAIN DISH RECIPES

Slow cooker lentil chilies & chickpea

Slow cooker lentil chilies & chickpea

Ingredients

1 cup dried chickpeas

2 qrt boiling water

2 cups sweet potatoes (chopped, 1/2 in. cubes)

1 cup lentils (uncooked)

1 cup purple onion (chopped)

5 cloves garlic (minced)

11/2 tsp ground cumin

1 tsp kosher salt

1/2 tsp chili powder

1/2 tsp ground cinnamon

1/4 tsp ground turmeric

1/2 cup golden raisins

21/2 cups low sodium vegetable broth

1/2 cup water

28 ozs tomatoes

Fresh cilantro (for topping)

Directions:

Place chickpeas in a saucepan, and add 2 quarts of boiling water. Cover and let stand for 1 hour; drain. Place cooked chickpeas in slow cooker. Add rest of the ingredients up to raisins. Mix well. Add liquids. Cover and cook on low for 6-8 hours. Serve sprinkling fresh cilantro.

Slow cooker sweet potato & vegetable curry

Ingredients

1 tsp canola oil

1/2 onions (medium, diced)

1 apple (diced)

2 tsp minced ginger

2 garlic cloves (minced)

1/4 cup mild curry paste

1 diced sweet potatoes

2 cups cauliflower florets (small)

21/2 cups low sodium chickpeas

14 ozs diced tomatoes (petite)

1 low sodium vegetable broth (14 oz.)

1/2 tsp ground pepper

1/4 tsp salt

1/2 cup lite coconut milk

11/2 cups chopped spinach leaves

Directions:

Heat the canola oil in a large nonstick skillet set over medium heat. Add the onion, apple and ginger, and cook until they are tender, 7 to 8 minutes. Add the garlic and cook for 30 seconds. Stir in the curry paste and cook, stirring, for 3 minutes. Transfer the onion mixture to a slow cooker. Add the sweet potato, cauliflower, chickpeas, diced tomatoes and vegetable broth to the slow cooker. Cook on HIGH for 6 hours, or until the vegetables are tender. Stir in the coconut milk and spinach, and heat. Serve.

Slow cooker quinoa with roasted poblanos

Ingredients

2 poblano peppers (medium, about ½ pound)

1 tbsp olive oil

1 diced onions

1 diced green pepper

2 cloves garlic (minced, about 2 teaspoons)

2 tsp ground cumin

1 tsp dried oregano

1/4 tsp smoked paprika

1/4 tsp ground cloves

1 tsp kosher salt

4 cups low sodium vegetable broth

4 cups cannellini beans (cooked white kidney bean)

3/4 cup quinoa

6 dashes Tabasco Pepper Sauce (optional)

Lime wedges

Sour cream

Shredded Monterey Jack cheese

Directions:

 Wash and dry whole peppers and place on a cookie sheet. Place in the oven and broil for 2-3 minutes, until the tops are blackened, then turn carefully with tongs and continue broiling until most sides are blistered and blackened. Remove blackened peppers from the oven and carefully tent a large piece of foil over the top. This helps the peppers to "sweat" and will make the skin easier to peel off .While the poblanos is cooling, assemble the rest of the chili. Heat the olive oil in a medium pan over medium heat. Add the diced onions and green peppers. Cook, stirring occasionally, until tender, 5-6 minutes. Add the garlic, oregano, cumin, smoked paprika, cloves, and salt. Cook, stirring, for one minute. Add a cup or so of broth and stir to make sure all the bits of flavor are scraped up into the broth. Carefully pour into the slow cooker along with the remaining vegetable broth, cannellini beans, quinoa, and Tabasco if using. Carefully peel the skin off of the poblanos and remove the stem. Finely dice and add to the Crock Pot. Stir gently to mix all of the ingredients together. Cook on low for 8 - 10 hours or on high for 3 - 4 hours until the quinoa is tender and the chili is relatively thick. Taste and add additional salt and pepper to taste. Scoop into bowls and squeeze a lime wedge over each serving. Garnish with additional toppings if desired.

Slow cooker sweet potato chili

Ingredients

2 sweet potatoes (peeled and in 2-inch chunks)

1 yellow onion (diced)

2 garlic cloves (minced)

15 ozs red kidney beans

1 red bell pepper (seeded and chopped)

141/2 ozs tomatoes

1 tbsp chili powder

1 tsp smoked paprika

1 tsp chili powder

1/2 tsp kosher salt

1 cup water

1/2 cup orange juice or water

Directions:

Use a 5-6 quart slow cooker. Peel and chunk the sweet potato and add to the pot. Add diced onion. Follow with the red bell pepper, can of tomatoes, the beans, garlic, and seasonings. Pour in OJ and water. Cover and cook on low for 6-8 hours, or until the onion is translucent and the sweet potato is fork-tender.

Crock pot bean and quinoa

Ingredients

16 ozs red beans (dried, pre-soaked overnight)

8 ozs dried black beans (pre-soaked overnight)

28 ozs canned chop tomatoes

2 tsp taco seasoning (natural)

10 ozs corn (frozen organic)

1 cup quinoa (uncooked)

2 tsp tomato purée (organic)

2 tsp salt

6 cups hot water

Directions:

Add all of the ingredients except corn and quinoa to the slow cooker. Set on high for 5-6 hours. After the time has passed, check to see if you need to add more liquid and how tender the beans are. If they are still too hard cook further for another hour otherwise add the quinoa and corn and cook further for 30 minutes. Leave slow cooker on warm setting until ready to serve.

Slow cooker Mediterranean stew

Ingredients

1 butternut squash (peeled, seeded, and cubed)

2 cups eggplant (cubed, with peel)

2 cups zucchini (cubed)

10 ozs frozen okra (thawed)

8 ozs tomato sauce

1 cup chopped onion

1 tomato (ripe, chopped)

1 carrot (sliced thin)

1/2 cup vegetable broth

1/3 cup raisins

1 clove garlic (chopped)

1/2 tsp ground cumin

1/2 tsp ground turmeric

1/4 tsp crushed red pepper

1/4 tsp ground cinnamon

1/4 tsp paprika

Directions:

In a slow cooker, combine butternut squash, eggplant, zucchini, okra, tomato sauce, onion, tomato, carrot, broth, raisins, and garlic. Season with cumin, turmeric, red pepper, cinnamon, and paprika. Cover, and cook on Low for 8 to 10 hours, or until vegetables are tender.

Black bean & rice in slow cooker

Black bean & rice in slow cooker

Ingredients

1 lb dried black beans

1 onions (large, chopped, 1 cup)

1 bell pepper (large, chopped, 1 1/2 cups)

5 cloves garlic (finely chopped)

2 bay leaves (dried)

141/2 ozs diced tomatoes

5 cups water

2 tsp olive oil

4 tsp ground cumin

2 tsp jalapeno chilies (finely chopped)

1 tsp salt

3 cups cooked rice

Directions:

In 3 1/2- to 6-quart slow cooker, mix all ingredients except rice. Cover; cook on High heat setting 6 to 8 hours. Remove bay leaves. Serve beans over rice.

Cauliflower chickpea curry

Ingredients

1 onion (chopped)

2 diced red chili peppers

1 tsp fresh ginger (peeled and minced)

1/4 cup cilantro stems (chopped, save tops for garnish)

1 head cauliflower (chopped)

2 orange bell pepper

1 can diced tomatoes

1 can light coconut milk

1 cans garbanzo (garbanzo beans)

1/2 cup hot sauce

6 cups rice (cooked)

1 lime slices

1 cup Greek yogurt (sour cream)

Directions:

Chop and dice all the vegetables. Put everything except the rice, lime and greek yogurt in the slow cooker. Cook on low for 6-8 hours or high for 4 hours. Cook rice according to package immediately before serving. To serve start with the rice in each bowl. Top with the vegetable curry, cilantro and a dollop of greek yogurt. Serve with a slice of lime on the side. Enjoy!

Slow cooker vegetarian chili

Ingredients

1 cup red kidney beans (dried)

1 cup great northern beans (dried)

1 cup black turtle beans (dried)

2 pepper (dried guajillo)

2 chipotle peppers (dried)

2 ancho chile peppers (dried)

1 green bell pepper (seeded and chopped)

1 yellow bell pepper (seeded and chopped)

1 orange bell pepper (seeded and chopped)

2 tsp olive oil

1 onion (chopped)

4 garlic cloves (minced)

1 tsp cumin (powdered)

2 tsp dried oregano

1/4 tsp cinnamon

1 tsp salt

28 ozs crushed tomatoes

4 cups vegetable broth

1 tbsp low sodium soy sauce

1 tsp hot sauce (optional)

Directions:

Add all the dried beans to a large bowl and cover with cold water. Allow to soak overnight. Drain the beans and set aside. Add the dried chili peppers in a small pot over medium heat and cover with water. Simmer for 10 minutes. Set aside. Heat the olive oil in a large pot over medium heat. Add the onions and garlic and cook until softened. Combine cumin, oregano, cinnamon and salt. Add to pot and stir for 30 seconds. Transfer to a slow cooker. Add pureed chilies, crushed tomatoes, beans, vegetable broth, and soy sauce. Stir to combine. For some added heat, add a teaspoon of your favorite hot sauce. Cover and cook on high for 3 to 4 hours. Season with salt and pepper if needed. Top with shredded cheese or sour cream, if desired.

Barbecued Tofu with Vegetables

Ingredients

Tofu (1 package, about 1 lb. extra-firm, regular)

1 onion (small, minced)

3 cloves garlic (minced)

2 tsp fresh ginger root (minced)

8 ozs tomato sauce (no salt added)

1/4 cup hoisin sauce

2 tsp seasoned rice wine vinegar

1/4 tsp vegan Worcestershire sauce

1 tbsp low sodium soy sauce

1 tbsp spicy brown mustard

1/4 tsp crushed red pepper

2 tsp molasses

1/4 tsp Chinese five-spice powder

1/8 tsp ground black pepper

Salt (to taste, optional)

2 tsp water

3 stalks broccoli

2 cubed zucchini

1/2 green bell pepper

8 ozs water chestnuts (sliced)

Directions:

Cut the tofu into 1/2-inch thick slices. Press lightly to remove some of the moisture from the tofu. Cut the slices into triangles or other shapes. Heat an oiled, non-stick skillet until hot, and place the tofu slices in it. Brown well on both sides. When they are done, place them in a crock pot that has been sprayed with non-stick spray. Set the crock pot to high heat and cover. Using the same skillet, sauté the onions, garlic, and ginger until the onion softens, about 3 minutes. Add the remaining ingredients and heat, stirring, until bubbly. Pour the sauce over the tofu and stir well to combine. Replace the cover and cook on high for 3 hours. Prepare the broccoli stalks Slice into 1/4-inch thick rounds. After the tofu has cooked for 3 hours, add the broccoli and other vegetables. Stir well to combine and cover tightly. Cook for about 1 more hour. Vegetables should be tender but not over-cooked. Serve over brown rice.

Vegan chickpea slow cooking stew

Ingredients

1 cans garbanzo

2 cups canned tomatoes

2/3 cup potatoes

1 cup onions (sliced)

Veggies (choice, diced)

1 tbsp curry powder

1 tbsp garlic powder

1 tbsp turmeric

Directions:

Combine all ingredients in slow cooker and cook on low for 6 to 8 hours.

Red bean & rice in slow cooker

Ingredients

1 lb small red beans

4 cups water

4 cloves garlic (minced)

1 onions (large, chopped, about 2 cups)

11/2 cups chopped celery

1 cup chopped green bell pepper

1 tbsp Worcestershire sauce

2 tsp Creole seasoning

Tabasco Pepper Sauce

Salt

Pepper

Direction:

Place dried beans in a large bowl and cover them with cold water by a couple of inches. Let soak for 8 hours or overnight. Place beans, garlic, chopped onion, and water in a large (8-quart) pot and bring to a boil. Reduce to a simmer and cover, simmer for 1 1/2 hours or until beans are tender. Let cool slightly Add the celery, bell peppers, Worcestershire and seasonings. Cover and cook for another hour or until the mixture gets thick. Season to taste with Tabasco sauce, salt and pepper. Serve over rice.

Crock pot spicy chickpea curry

Ingredients

15 ozs garbanzo (drained)

1 tbsp curry powder

1/4 tsp garam masala (mix of cloves, cinnamons, cardamoms)

1/4 tsp coriander (powder)

1/2 tsp cumin

1/2 tsp seasoning (green)

2 tsp water

2 tsp canola oil

1/2 onions (finely chopped)

1/2 tsp salt

3 cups water

Directions:

Take a small bowl, mix curry powder, garam masala, coriander powder, cumin, green seasoning and 2 tablespoon water to form a paste. In a medium size pot, heat oil over medium fire. When oil is hot add curry paste and onion and cook for 3-5 minutes, stirring occasionally. If the paste becomes dry, about a tablespoon of water to prevent it from burning. Next add chick pea, salt and remaining 4 cups of water. Cook until the chick peas are tender. Add water as needed. Serve hot with cilantro.

Slow cooker vegetable stew

Ingredients

1 eggplant (large, chopped and peeled)

1 yellow onion (chopped)

2 green pepper (seeded and cut into pieces)

1 can tomatoes (diced or stewed, 14.5 oz)

1 tbsp minced garlic

1/2 cup extra-virgin olive oil

2 zucchini (small, chopped)

2 tsp fresh basil (chopped)

Salt

Pepper

Directions:

Put the eggplant in a colander and sprinkle it with salt so the moisture is removed and drains away. Put the eggplant, onion, peppers, tomatoes and garlic in the slow cooker. Pour the olive oil over the top and stir. Cook on high for 1½ hours or low for 2 to 3. Stir in the zucchini. Cover and cook on high for another 1½ hours on high or 2 to 3 hours on low minutes before it is done, add the fresh basil and the salt and pepper. Serve with crumbled feta cheese or sour cream if desired.

Slow cooked veggie chili

Ingredients

1 stick cooking spray

141/2 ozs diced tomatoes

8 ozs tomato sauce

15 ozs Ranch Style Beans

15 ozs red kidney beans

1 yellow onion (small, chopped)

1 green bell pepper (medium, chopped)

1 cup frozen whole kernel corn

2 carrots (medium, sliced)

1 tbsp Chili Powder

1/2 tsp ground red pepper

Directions:

Spray inside of 4-quart slow cooker with cooking spray. Place remaining ingredients in slow cooker; stir to combine. Cover; cook on HIGH 1-1/2 to 2 hours or on low 3 to 4 hours. Serve.

Mint rice with slowed coked lentils

Ingredients

2 cups lentils

10 cups low sodium vegetable broth

2 tbsps curry powder

1 tsp chili flakes

1 tsp fresh ginger (chopped)

2 bell pepper (seeded and chopped)

1 onion (chopped)

4 garlic cloves (chopped)

2 cups baby carrots

Pepper

Salt

1 cup long grain brown rice

1 tbsp olive oil

2 tbsps fresh mint (chopped, plus extra for garnishing)

Directions:

Place lentils, stock, curry powder, chili flakes, fresh ginger, onion, garlic, carrots and potatoes in a slow cooker. Cook for 4-6 hours on high or 6-8 hours on low or until lentils are cooked and carrots and potatoes are tender. Season to taste with salt and pepper.

To prepare the mint rice-In a large saucepan, combine the two cups of water, olive oil and the rice.Bring to a boil over medium-high heat. Reduce heat to a low and cover.Cook for about 35-40 minutes, or until all the water is absorbed. Remove saucepan from heat and allow cooling for 10 minutes, covered. Toss rice with the mint.

To complete the dish-Spoon some of the mint rice onto a plate and top with the lentils. Garnish with chopped mint on top and enjoy.

Blackeyed peas & Okra in a crock pot

Ingredients

60 ozs black-eyed peas

15 ozs kidney beans

1/2 cup chopped onion

1 cup green pepper (chopped)

1 cup chopped celery

16 ozs okra (frozen sliced)

28 ozs diced tomatoes

Directions:

Combine all ingredients in crock pot. Stir well, cover and cook on low for 8 hours.

Vegan Spaghetti squash

Vegan spaghetti squash

Ingredients

32 ozs spaghetti squash

11/2 cups sun-dried tomatoes in oil (chopped)

1 onion (medium, chopped)

1 cup celery (chopped)

2 garlic cloves (minced)

8 ozs sliced mushrooms

431/2 ozs chopped tomatoes

2/3 cup dry white wine

1 tsp fennel seeds (dried)

11/2 tsps basil

1/2 tsp oregano

Salt

Black pepper

Directions:

Combine all the ingredients in a slow cooker. Cover and cook on low for 6 to 8 hours.

Indian style lentils

Ingredients

1/2 cup lentils (masoor)

1/2 cup lentils (moong)

1/2 tsp tumeric (powder)

1 tbsp butter

1 tbsp olive oil

1/2 tsp cumin seed

1/2 tsp mustard seeds

1/2 onions (finely chopped)

1 chilli

2 cloves garlic (grated)

1 in fresh ginger (grated)

11/2 tsps salt (according to taste)

1 tsp garam masala

1/2 tsp paprika

1/4 cans plum tomatoes

1 handful fresh cilantro (chopped)

Directions:

Boil the lentils in the slow cooker for about 3-4 hours or till the lentils are tender and cooked. Then add the remaining ingredients and allow it to boil for another hour and garnish with cilantro.

Potato & kidney bean crock pot curry

Ingredients

4 potatoes

28 ozs rotel tomatoes (& chilies)

31 ozs kidney beans

2 white onions (chopped)

2 tbsps olive oil

1 tbsp curry powder

1 tsp cayenne

1/2 tsp cardamom (optional)

1/2 tsp ginger (optional)

Directions:

Heat olive oil in a saucepan or skillet. Add spices, saute for 1 minute. Add onions and saute for 2 - 5 minutes. Add both cans of Rotel. Pour mixture into crockpot. Add potatoes and canned beans to crockpot. Allow to crock on low for 6 - 9 hours or on high for 3 - 5 hours, depending on your crockpot. Serve over rice.

SIDE DISH RECIPES

Garlic parmesan potatoes

Ingredients

3 lbs gold potatoes (baby Dutch, halved)

2 tbsps olive oil

2 tbsps unsalted butter

4 cloves garlic (minced)

1/2 tsp dried oregano

1/2 tsp dried basil

1/2 tsp dried dill

Kosher salt

Ground black pepper

1/4 cup freshly grated parmesan

2 tbsps fresh parsley leaves (chopped)

Directions:

Lightly coat the inside of a slow cooker with nonstick spray. Place potatoes, olive oil, butter, garlic, oregano, basil and dill into the slow cooker; season with salt and pepper, to taste. Cover and cook on low heat for 4-5 hours or high heat for 2-3 hours or until tender.Serve immediately, sprinkled with Parmesan and garnished with parsley, if desired.

Yellow squash

Ingredients

2 tbsps olive oil

1 onion (medium, halved and thinly sliced)

4 yellow squash (8 ounces each, thinly sliced)

Coarse salt

Ground pepper

Directions:

In a large pot, heat oil over medium-low. Add onion, squashes, and 2 tablespoons water. Season with salt and pepper, and toss well. Cover, and cook, stirring occasionally, until soft, 30 to 35 minutes.

Glazed carrots

Ingredients

2 lbs baby carrots

4 tbsps butter (cut into tablespoon chunks)

1/2 cup brown sugar (plus a little extra)

Directions:

Spray slow cooker with non-stick cooking spray. Place in carrots. Top with butter and sugar .Cook on high for about 4-5 hours (or low for 8-9 hours). After about 2 hours give the carrots a good stir. Stir again after another hour and every hour until done. Take cooked carrots out of slow cooker and sprinkle a little extra sugar onto carrots while they are still hot.

Sweet potato casserole

Sweet potato casserole

Ingredients

58 ozs sweet potatoes

1/3 cup butter (melted)

2 tbsps white sugar

2 tbsps brown sugar

1 tbsp orange juice

1/2 cup milk

1/3 cup chopped pecans

1/3 cup brown sugar

2 tbsps all-purpose flour

2 tsps butter (melted)

Directions:

Lightly grease a slow cooker. In a large bowl, blend sweet potatoes, 1/3 cup butter, white sugar and 2 tablespoons brown sugar. Beat in orange juice and milk. Transfer this mixture to the prepared casserole dish. In a small bowl, combine pecans, 1/3 cup brown sugar, flour and 2 tablespoons butter. Spread the mixture over the sweet potatoes. Cover the slow cooker and cook on HIGH for 3 to 4 hours.

Garlic mashed potatoes

Ingredients

3 lbs red potato (chopped)

1/4 cup unsalted butter

4 cloves garlic (crushed and peeled)

Kosher salt

Ground black pepper

1/2 cup sour cream

1/3 cup freshly grated parmesan

2 tbsps milk (or more, as needed)

1/2 tsp dried thyme

1/2 tsp dried oregano

1/2 tsp dried basil

1/4 tsp grated nutmeg (freshly)

2 tbsps chopped fresh chives

Directions:

Lightly coat the inside of a slow cooker with nonstick spray. Place potatoes, butter, garlic and 1/4 cup water into the slow cooker; season with salt and pepper, to taste. Cover and cook on low heat for 7-8 hours or high heat for 3-4 hours, or until tender. Add sour cream, Parmesan, milk, thyme, oregano, basil and nutmeg. Using an electric mixer fitted with the paddle attachment, blend potatoes until light and fluffy, about 2-3 minutes. If the mixture is too thick, add more milk as needed until desired consistency is reached. Serve immediately, garnished with chives, if desired.

Slow cooked green bean

Ingredients

1/4 cup extra-virgin olive oil

2 cups yellow onion (thinly sliced)

11/2 lbs green beans (clipped and cleaned)

3 garlic cloves (minced)

1 tsp pomegranate molasses

1/2 lemon

1 tsp allspice

14 ozs chopped tomatoes

2 tsps tomato paste

Ground pepper

Kosher salt

Direction:

Place a large heavy bottomed pot over medium heat. Add the olive oil and once it is hot add the onions. Season the onions with a pinch of salt and some pepper. Add the garlic and once it becomes fragrant add the allspice and sugar. Then add the beans and stir them to coat with the oil. Now add the rest of the ingredients and stir to combine. Cook on medium until you hear the pot sizzling then reduce the heat to low, cover, and cook for an hour remembering to stir about every twenty minutes. They may take longer the hour but not much. Taste, adjust the salt and pepper and serve.

Root vegetables in a crock pot

Ingredients

2 purple onions (sliced)

1/2 cup coconut oil

1/2 cup vegetable broth

1 tsp dried basil

1 tsp oregano

2 sweet potatoes (medium, chopped into small pieces)

3 carrots (chopped into small pieces)

2 parsnips (medium, chopped into small pieces)

Directions:

Add all of the ingredients to your slow cooker. Cover and cook on low for 5 hours or until vegetables are tender.

Mushroom-Barley Risotto

Ingredients

2 tbsps olive oil

1 cup yellow onion (chopped)

12 ozs crimini mushrooms (cleaned and sliced)

3 tbsps fresh parsley (chopped)

1 tbsp chopped fresh thyme

2 cloves garlic (minced)

1 cup pearl barley

6 cups vegetable broth

1 tbsp unsalted butter

1/2 cup parmesan cheese (shredded)

Directions:

Heat the olive oil in a large, heavy-bottomed saucepan over medium heat. Saute onion until it starts to brown, about 5 minutes. Add the mushrooms and saute until they have released all of their liquid and are golden brown, about 10 minutes. You can add 1 to 3 tablespoons of water if they start to stick. Stir in the herbs and garlic, then add the barley and stir to coat for 1 minute. Add 4 cups of the broth and bring to a boil over high heat. Cook for 15 minutes, stirring occasionally, until most of the liquid is absorbed. Reduce the heat to medium and add more broth, ½ cup at a time, stirring until each addition is absorbed, until the barley is tender.Remove the pan from the heat and add the butter and cheese, stirring until incorporated. Season with salt and pepper, to taste.

Onions caramalized in the crock pot

Ingredients

8 yellow onion (large)

3 tbsps butter

3 tbsps olive oil

1 pinch salt

2 tsps balsamic vinegar (optional)

Directions:

Set the crockpot on high heat and add the butter and olive oil. Slice the onions and fill the crockpot with them. Add a pinch of salt. Toss the onions to coat with the oils. Leave the lid OFF and walk away.Stir the onions occasionally, scraping the sides each time. Cook this till 8 hours. When the onions are slightly brown and softened, add the balsamic vinegar.

Slow cooking loaded baked potatoes

Slow cooking loaded baked potatoes

Ingredients

4 russet potatoes (medium)

2 tbsps olive oil

10 ozs cremini mushrooms (trimmed and quartered)

1 bunch broccoli (cut into small florets, stalks peeled and cut into 1/2-inch pieces)

Pepper

Salt

1/2 cup vegetable broth

2/3 cup low-fat plain yogurt (room temperature)

Directions:

Wrap each potato in foil and place in a 5-to-6-quart slow cooker. Cover and cook on low until potatoes are tender, 8 hours. In a large skillet, heat oil over medium-high. Add mushrooms and cook 2 minutes, then add broccoli and season with salt and pepper. Cook, stirring frequently, until broccoli is crisp-tender, 8 minutes. Split potatoes, scoop out flesh, and transfer to a medium bowl, reserving skins. Add broth and yogurt to bowl, then season with salt and pepper and stir until combined; divide among potato skins. Top each stuffed potato with broccoli mixture.

DESSERT RECIPES

Slow cooked apple crisp

Ingredients

1 cup all-purpose flour

1/2 cup light brown sugar

1/2 cup white sugar

1/2 tsp ground cinnamon

1/4 tsp ground nutmeg

1 pinch salt

1/2 cup butter (cut into pieces)

1 cup chopped walnuts

1/3 cup white sugar (or to taste)

1 tbsp corn starch

1/2 tsp ground ginger

1/2 tsp ground cinnamon

6 cups apples (peeled, cored and chopped)

2 tbsps lemon juice

Directions:

Mix flour, brown sugar, 1/2 cup of white sugar, 1/2 teaspoon cinnamon, nutmeg, and salt together in a bowl. Combine butter with the flour mixture using fingers or a fork until coarse crumbs form. Stir in walnuts and set aside. Whisk together 1/3 cup sugar, cornstarch, ginger, and 1/2 teaspoon cinnamon. Place the apples in a slow cooker, stir in the cornstarch mixture; toss with lemon juice. Sprinkle the walnut crumb topping on top. Cover and cook on High for 2 hours or Low for 4 hours, until apples are tender. Partially uncover the slow cooker to allow the topping to harden, about 1 hour.

Crock pot Fudge

Ingredients

21/2 cups chocolate chips

1/4 cup coconut milk (canned, not in a carton)

1/4 cup honey (raw mild)

1 dash sea salt

1 tsp pure vanilla extract

Direction:

Add chocolate chips, coconut milk, coconut sugar, and salt, and coconut oil, stir to combine. Next, cover and cook on low 2 hours without stirring. It's important that lid remain on during the 2 hours. After 2 hours, turn the slow cooker off, uncover, and add vanilla. IMPORTANT; do not stir fudge mixture at this point. Allow cooling to room temperature, or it reaches 110 degrees with a candy thermometer. Once cooled, use a large spoon, stir vigorously for 5-10 minutes until it loses some the gloss. Lightly oil an 8"x8" square pan. Pour fudge into pan, cover and refrigerate 4 hours or until firm.

Crock pot Rice Pudding

Ingredients

8 cups milk

1 cup long grain white rice

1 cup sugar

1/4 cup heavy cream (or half and half)

2 tsps vanilla

1/2 tsp cinnamon

1/4 tsp salt

Direction:

I used a 4 quart slow cooker. Spray the stoneware insert with cooking spray, then combine the milk, rice, and sugar. Stir well and cook on low for 4-6 hours, or high for about 4. It took longer than I expected for my rice to become bite-tender---I did low for 3 hours, then high for another 2. When the rice is tender, mix in a large mixing bowl, the cream, vanilla, cinnamon, and salt. Scoop a 1/2 cup of the hot rice mixture into the mixing bowl and whisk. Keep adding 1/2 cup at a time of the rice and milk mixture into the cream bowl until about half of the milk and rice mixture is gone from the slow cooker. Then pour everything back into the pot. Stir well.Cover and cook on high for 1 hour. Stir well, then take the lid off of the cooker and unplug it. When the rice pudding is room temperature, you can refrigerate it. Some people like their pudding hot or warm, and some prefer it chilled.

Sugar candied cinnamon & almonds

Sugar candied cinnamon & almonds

Ingredients

11/2 cups sugar

11/2 cups light brown sugar

3 tbsps cinnamon

1/8 tsp salt

2 tsps vanilla

41/2 cups raw almond

1/4 cup water

Direction

Spray your slow cooker with non-stick spray and set aside.In a large bowl, add the sugar, brown sugar, cinnamon, vanilla and salt. Whisk together. Pour the almonds mixture and toss them around to coat thoroughly. Pour the entire mixture into the slow cooker and turn to low. Cook for 3-3.5 hours, stirring every 20 minutes. It will look like not much is happening for a long time but your house will smell good! After 3 hours, pour in the ¼ cup of water and stir well. This is going to make the crunchy coating and things will start looking right. Leave in the slow cooker for another 20-30 minutes. Meanwhile, line a baking sheet with parchment paper. When done, pour the almonds onto the prepared baking sheet and separate any that stuck together. Let them cool slightly to harden then enjoy!

Crock pot banana foster

Ingredients

4 bananas (peeled and sliced)

4 tbsps butter (melted)

1 cup brown sugar (packed)

1/4 cup rum

1 tsp vanilla extract

1/2 tsp ground cinnamon

1/4 cup chopped walnuts

1/4 cup shredded coconut

Directions:

Layer sliced bananas in the bottom of a slow cooker. Combine butter, brown sugar, rum, vanilla and cinnamon in a small bowl; pour over bananas. Cover and cook on low for 2 hours. Top bananas with walnuts and coconut during the last 30 minutes of cooking.

Donut Bread pudding

Ingredients

8 cake donuts (not the raised kind*)

5 cups milk

3/4 cup sugar

1/2 tsp nutmeg

1/8 tsp mace

Direction:

You can use day-old french or Italian bread, but increase the sugar to 1 cup, the nutmeg to 1 tsp and the mace to 1/4 tsp--these 2 spices are the standard "donut" spices so the overall pudding will taste like cake donuts. Cut donuts into small pieces about 1 inch. Place in crockpot. In a large bowl, whisk in the milk, sugar and spices. Pour over donuts in crock pot. Cover and cook on HI 4 hours, LOW 6-8 hours.

Slow cooked tapioca pudding

Ingredients

4 cups milk (any variety)

2/3 cup white sugar

1/2 cup small pearl tapioca (not instant)

2 tsps vanilla

Directions

Add to the milk, sugar, vanilla, and tapioca. Cover and crock on HIGH 3 hours, or on LOW for 6 hours.

Make sure to stir often while cooking. Serve warm and sprinkle with cinnamon, if desired

Crock pot nutella chocolate chip cake

Ingredients

2 cups all-purpose flour

1/2 tsp cream of tartar

1/4 tsp kosher salt

1 cup unsalted butter

1 cup granulated sugar

1 tbsp vanilla extract

3 tbsps Nutella

1/2 cup chocolate chips

Direction:

Spray in the inside of a slow-cooker insert with cooking spray and line it with parchment paper that comes at least three inches up the side. Stir together the flour, tartar and salt in a small bowl and set aside.Melt the butter in a large bowl and stir in the sugar and vanilla extract, then add the flour mixture until just combined. Stir in the chocolate chips. Pour the mixture into the slow-cooker and spread it evenly with a spatula. Dollop the nutella on top of the batter and use a butter knife to swirl it into the batter. Cook on high heat for three hours, or until a cake tester comes out clean.

Apple cranberry crisp

Ingredients

5 apples (large, sliced, peel if desired)

1/2 cup dried cranberries

1/2 cup brown sugar (divided)

2 tbsps lemon juice

1/2 cup flour

1/4 tsp salt

1/4 tsp ground cinnamon

1/4 cup butter (cold, sliced)

1/4 cup oats

Directions:

Spray inside of slow cooker with non-stick cooking spray. Combine inside slow cooker the following: sliced apples, dried cranberries, 1/4 cup brown sugar and lemon juice, stir ingredients to combine. In small bowl combine: flour, salt, remaining 1/4 cup brown sugar, salt & ground cinnamon. Cut in cold butter with 2 knives or pasty blender. When pea sized pieces have formed stir in oats. Dump flour/oat mixture on top of apple mixture in slow cooker. Cover. Cook on high 2 hours (times/temp may vary). Serve warm with vanilla ice cream or freshly whipped cream.

Crock pot berry cobbler

Ingredients

11/4 cups all-purpose flour (divided)

2 tbsps sugar (divided)

1 tsp baking powder

1/4 tsp ground cinnamon

1/4 cup fat free milk

2 tbsps canola oil

1/8 tsp salt

2 cups frozen raspberries

2 cups frozen blueberries

Low-fat vanilla frozen yogurt (optional)

Directions:

In a large bowl, combine 1 cup flour, 2 tablespoons sugar, baking powder and cinnamon. Combine the, milk and oil; stir into dry ingredients just until moistened (batter will be thick). Spread batter evenly into a 5-qt. slow cooker coated with cooking spray. In a large bowl, combine the salt and remaining flour and sugar; add berries and toss to coat. Spread over batter. Cover and cook on high for 2 to 2-1/2 hours or until a toothpick inserted into cobbler comes out clean. Serve with frozen yogurt if desired.

Conclusion

I hope this book gave you some useful insights on what is Slow Cooking and how it can be used to prepare tasty DASH diet recipes that can help you lower your blood pressure and reduce your weight. I am sure you'll find the slow cooker recipes in this book easy to prepare and delicious to eat.

Please remember that this is not a crash diet that you can follow for a week, shed a few pounds and go back to your old diet habits. Your goal should be to make DASH diet a lifelong habit. This would help you to stay healthy and enjoy the benefits of the diet in the long run. This is not just for people with hypertension. The entire family can follow this healthy diet plan as it is easy and safe to follow. Consulting your doctor before starting the diet is highly recommended.

Thank you!

Thank you for buying and downloading my book DASH Diet Slow Cooker Recipes! Finally, if you enjoyed this book, please take the time to share your thoughts and post a review on Amazon. It'd be greatly appreciated!

This feedback will help me to continue writing the kind of books that would give you the maximum value and results. Thank you once again and good luck!

Don't forget to claim your free bonus here: http://dietcookbooks.co/dashdiet/

FREE BONUS!

To help you start your DASH diet and stay committed to your diet plan, I've put together a DASH Diet Hamper which includes the following:

a. Audio version of the Amazon Bestseller book **"Blood Pressure Solution" by Jessica Robbins**
b. **7 day vegetarian meal plan** for DASH Diet
c. Tips to reduce sodium
d. DASH Diet Shopping List
e. Tips to get started with the DASH Diet
f. Sodium Content Chart of various foods

Additional Bonus!

Receive the first copies of all my diet and cookbooks as soon as they get published for FREE!

Get Access to the FREE DASH Diet Hamper HERE: http://dietcookbooks.co/dashdiet/

Recommended Reading

I highly recommend you to read some of these other great resources on DASH Diet & Slow Cooker Recipes:

365 Days of Crock Pot Recipes by Emma Katie

Slow Cooking for Two by Mendocino Press

365 Days of Slow Cooking Recipes by Emma Katie

Dash Diet Slow Cooker Recipes

DASH Diet for Vegetarians by Renee Sanders

The DASH Diet Weight Loss Solution by Marla Keller

The Everyday DASH Diet Cookbook by Marla Keller

The DASH Diet Action Plan by Marla Keller

DASH Diet Slow Cooker Recipes by Maddie Bridges

The DASH Diet for Beginners by Gina Crawford

Disclaimer

This eBook, DASH Diet Slow Cooker Recipes is written with an intention to serve as a purely informational and educational resource. It is not intended to be a medical advice or a medical guide. Although proper care has been taken to ensure the validity and reliability of the information provided in this eBook, readers are advised to exert caution before using any of the information, suggestions, and methods described in this book.

The writer does not advocate the use of any of the suggestions, diets, and health programs mentioned in this book. This book is not intended to take the place of a medical professional, a doctor and physician. The information in this book should not be used without the explicit advice from medically trained professionals especially in cases where urgent diagnosis and medical treatment is required. The author or publisher cannot be held responsible for any personal or commercial damage in misinterpreting or misunderstanding any part of the book.

Made in the USA
Lexington, KY
12 September 2015